I AM BLESSED DAILY

Daily positive declaration to change your life

Copyright © 2016 Selina Essumang

All rights reserved. No part of this publication may be produced, distributed, or transmitted in any form or by any means, including photocopying, recording, or other electronic or mechanical methods, without the prior written permission of the publisher, except in the case of brief quotations embodied in critical reviews and certain other non-commercial uses permitted by copyright law.

For permission requests, write to the publisher, addressed "Attention: Permissions Coordinator" at the email address below:
Life and Success Media Ltd
email: info@abookinsideyou.com
www. abookinsideyou.com

Unless otherwise stated, all scripture quotations are taken from the Holy Bible, New Living Translation (NLT). Other versions cited are NIV, NKJV, AMP and KJV. Quotations marked NIV are taken from the HOLY BIBLE, NEW INTERNATIONAL VERSION. Copyright © 1973, 1978, 1984 by International Bible Society. Used by permission of Hodder and Stoughton Ltd, a member of the Hodder Headline Plc Group. All rights reserved. "NIV" is a registered trademark of International Bible Society. UK trademark number 1448790.

Quotations marked KJV are from the Holy Bible, King James Version.
ISBN: 978-1-907402-79-1

Cover design: miadesign.com

Acknowledgement

To my spiritual father and mother Rev. Dr. David Antwi & Rev. Awo Antwi of Kharis Ministries for their encouragement and prayers.

My husband Maxwell and children Sadie & Cedric for being there for me all the time. Also to my dear friend and sister Motolani.

God bless you all immensely in Jesus name.

DEDICATION

I dedicate this book to God Almighty for giving me the insight and knowledge in completing His Project. As He had used me as His vessel.

TABLE OF CONTENTS

Introduction 6

Positive Confession... 7

Daily proclamation to change your life 8

Readers Personal Notes 41

I am blessed daily 2016 calendar 42

Author's Note.. 43

About the Author 44

Introduction

This book will enlighten your knowledge on the journey to prosperity. The power of positive declaration will enable you speak life by faith to unlock your spiritual blessings. Faith is what you need as a believer in your walk with God.

Whatsoever, you believe in your heart must be spoken in FAITH. "Faith is what gets the job done"
(Dr. David Antwi).

A Believer who speaks without FAITH is like pouring water in a basket. All the hard work is in vain and nothing will be achieved.

As you hear the word and knowing the sovereignty of God, believe and speak it in faith to uproot, break and unlock your destiny to receive.

I believe this book will serve its purpose in your life as you declare in FAITH.

God bless and empower you in Jesus name.

POSITIVE CONFESSION

WHAT DO YOU KNOW ABOUT POSITIVE CONFESSION? HOW OFTEN DO YOU SPEAK POSITIVE WORDS TO CHANGE YOUR LIFE?
WE ARE OVER-COMERS BY THE WORD OF OUR CONFESSIONS THROUGH OUR FAITH. 1 John 5:4

THEREFORE, THERE IS A NEED TO SPEAK LIFE INTO YOUR LIFE AND HAVE FAITH WHEN YOU DECLARE BECAUSE IT SHALL SURELY BE MANIFESTED.

DON'T BE HESITANT TO BLESS YOUR FUTURE WITH THE POWER OF THE WORD GOD HAS GIVEN US.

DAILY PROCLAMATION TO CHANGE YOUR LIFE.

1. I take back all my blessings which were hidden from me by the enemy. I am going to excel and take dominion over my possessions. I will multiply and replenish in destiny as God has position me. (Genesis 1:28).

2. I declare that, the blessings God has commanded upon me and my children (names) will never cease. It shall be fruitful in Jesus name (Leviticus 25:21).

3. Father, I thank you for blessing my children (name them) and I, I also give you praise for making us great and a point of blessing to other people's lives. (Genesis 12:2).

4. Lord you said, you will enlarge my boarders and I shall eat all that I wanted because you would provide for me and my family. (Deuteronomy 12:20).

5. I declare today, as it has been written that the promise belong to me and my children, I take it by divine force in the name of Jesus (Acts 2:39).

6. Father I believe I am blessed because all your promise are Ye and Amen. (2 Corinthians 1:20).

7. My God is forever good and He will fulfil His promises to me because I have faith, I will never be a failure in Jesus name. (2 Samuel 7:28).

8. Thank you Heavenly Father for welcoming me with blessings and a crown of pure gold on my head, I am forever grateful. (Psalm 21:3).

9. I decree and declare that, from today the blessings of God will find existence in me and my children's life (mention their names) to enable me (us) fulfil my (our) destiny (Proverb 10:6).

10. Today, I shall abound in blessings because the word of God says so (Proverbs 28:20).

11. I zoom into my destiny now in the mighty name of Jesus to take my spiritual blessings in heavenly places because my time is due (Ephesians 1:3).

12. I will never lack, I will be fruitful and will multiple in everything I do in Jesus name (Genesis 1:22).

13. Lord, I thank you for blessing and multiplying my seed as the stars of the heavens and as the sand upon the sea shore and making me great in Jesus name (Genesis 22:17).

14. My children will do signs and wonders because there has been transference of blessing in the mighty name of Jesus. (Genesis 25:11).

15. I thank you Father, for your provision through your blessings which has made way bringing forth fruits for more years to come (Leviticus 25:21).

16. In Jesus name, I am blessed and protected, all glory to God. (Numbers 6:23).

17. Thank you Lord for changing the mind-set of the enemy from curses to blessings in Jesus name (Numbers 23:20).

18. Lord, bless and favor me this morning, afternoon and evenings as I go to work (name place) (Joshua 22:6).

19. Father, I thank you and I will forever be grateful that you are blessing me with my Boaz (Ruth2:4).

20. I pray this day that my Lord would bless me indeed and keep me from all evil in Jesus name Amen (1 Chronicles 4:10).

21. Am forever grateful to you oh Lord, for your goodness and your covenant promise that has change my life forever in Jesus name (1 Chronicles 17:26).

22. I degree and declare that the blessing of God over my entire House-hold will be overwhelming and God's hedge around me and my family will be beyond understanding in the mighty name of Jesus (Job 1:10).

23. Glory be to your Holy name oh Lord, because you have been my rock and my salvation I will give you thanks all the time. (Psalm 18:46).

24. I am blessed everyday of my life because God has given me strength and a peace of mind (Psalm 29: 11).

25. Because I trusted in the Lord I am blessed in Jesus name. Amen (Psalm 34:8).

26. I claim by shouting out in faith that, what the Locust and Cankerworm ate in my life has been restored in Jesus name (Joel 2:7).

27. The fruit of my womb are bless and they shall be great in Jesus name (Luke 1:42).

28. I praise thee oh LORD, for making a barren woman like me (mention name) to become a joyful mother and for blessing me to sit with the prince and princess (Psalm 113: 8-9).

29. With faith I declare, my God will watch over his word in my life until it is accomplished in Jesus name (Isaiah 7:22).

30. Almighty God, I thank you that you have delivered me like you delivered Shadrach, Meshach and Abednego. (Daniel 2:23-26).

31. I am going out rejoicing because today my God has made me victorious over my enemies (Nehemiah 6:16).

32. Father, I thank you for the authority and enormous power you have given me (Psalm 8:6).

33. I am blessed because I am a child of most high God exercising wisdom concerning all things that are done on earth. (Ecclesiastes 1:13).

34. My songs of praise will go up high to my Lord today, because He has done excellent things in me and my family's lives. (Isaiah 12:5).

35. Lord Jesus, I thank you for my provision all the time and by faith I declare that I lack nothing in Jesus name (Matthew 6: 32).

36. I give you praise for blessing and raising me up of the dust by grace. You lifted me out from the dunghill and set me among princes to inherit the throne (1 Samuel 2:8).

37. Glory to your holy name, my heart will rejoice because it has seek the Lord and He has dealt with me well (1 Chronicles 16:10).

38. Father, I thank you for having made the glory of my latter days greater than my former and crowning it with your PEACE (Haggai 2:9).

39. I worship you oh Lord, for setting your fire around the walls of my household with your glorious mist (Zechariah 2: 5).

40. I thank you Lord Jesus for giving me a bright life and a future without toil like the lilies of the valley (Luke 12:27).

41. I rejoice because I know my God will never put me to shame, I believe with all my heart because He live by his word (Isaiah 54:4).

42. I degree and declare that, my God is taking me out of affliction and I am coming out of captivity now in Jesus name (Exodus 6:6).

43. I am favored and blessed in all my endeavors in Jesus name (Exodus 3:22).

44. I declare in the name of Jesus, that the enemy is put under my feet now (Exodus 9:11).

45. I praise God today for the release of my destiny helpers. (Exodus 12:36).

46. I will fear not because the enemies I see today, I will see them no more declared the Lord of host and I believe (Exodus 14.13).

47. God I thank you for your blessings that will never change in my life (Numbers 23:20).

48. Father, I thank you for your restoration, provision and most of all your blessings upon me and my seeds. (Isaiah 44:3).

49. The day of the Lord has come to do great things in my life (name children and others). I connect myself to receive in the mighty name of Jesus (Joel 1:15).

50. I believe that by faith, my tongue will always confess positive things and bring blessings to my life in Jesus name (James 3:6).

51. By faith, I will be victorious through all the troubles that comes my way, the enemies will be put to shame in Jesus name Amen (Hebrews 11:29).

52. Lord, I am not worthy but by faith, I receive my healing because your word has come forth (Matthew 8:8).

53. I can do all things through Christ who strengthens me, by faith am doing it now in Jesus name (Philippians 4:13).

54. I decree through the blood of Jesus that, I am free from any yoke and bondage. I confess liberty into my future now (Galatians 5:1).

55. In the mighty name of Jesus, I set myself free from any fellowships that would bring shame into my life right now (2 Corinthians 6: 14).

56. I will be favored by kings and Queens. My days of servant-hood has ended in Jesus name (2 Samuel 14:22).

57. I survived today because the GRACE of God abounds in my life and has given me everlasting PEACE through Jesus Christ. (1 Corinthians 1:3).

58. I thank God that in all the trails, He has made me stronger and standing firm through His GRACE (2 Timothy 2:1).

59. I rejoice because my Lord has fought my battles for me and has given me PEACE of mind (Exodus 14: 14).

60. I thank God for showing me mercy and favor in the sight of my divine destiny helpers as He did for Jacob (Genesis 39:21).

61. I give God thanks and praise because He made me not to rely on myself or anyone else but in HIM ALONE (2 Corinthians 1:9).

62. In spite of all the troubles and persecution, God will show Himself faithful and will never fail me (2 Corinthians 1:10).

63. In the name of Jesus I declare that, as I live by faith and not by sight everything my heart desires is done (2 Corinthians 5:7).

64. Father, I thank you for making me a new creation, in spite of my sins you have given me a second chance in life. (2 Corinthians 5: 17).

65. I declare by faith that, God's presence is with me and He will give me rest. So it does not matter the storm I am confident in Jesus name. (Exodus 33: 14).

66. It's by the mercies of God that, I am not consumed by the enemies and I declare that I shall never be consumed in the mighty name of Jesus (Lamentation 3:22).

67. By faith, I decree and declare that, as my soul seek the Lord, He will forever be good to me and takes care of me (Lamentation 3: 24).

68. My God will never lie to me, therefore by faith I am content to wait patiently (Job 6:28).

69. In the mighty name of Jesus, I shall not be afraid of the enemy's destructions when it comes because my God has already taken care of it. (Job 5: 21).

70. By the grace of God any iniquity in my tongue is wipe off now in Jesus name. (Job 6:30).

71. I decree the favor of Esther onto me and my children's lives. We shall never lack and everywhere we go, the favor of God will speak on our behalf in Jesus name (Esther 7: 4).

72. In the name of Jesus my tongue shall always proclaim good things that will bear good fruit into my life. (Psalm 34: 13 & 1 Peter 3: 10).

73. In the mighty name of Jesus, I declare my salvation has come and I am no more in bondage (Isaiah 62: 11).

74. As for me and my household, our future is in the hands of God. He has made our path perfect from all troubles (Psalm 31:15).

75. I decree and declare in the mighty name of Jesus that, there shall be a performance in my life (name someone) because I trust and have faith in the Lord of Host. (Luke 1: 45).

76. I thank God for his provision and empowering me and my family's lives. I step out today with gladness of heart. (Joel 2:19).

77. I declare that I am a good tree and I will bear good fruit, there would be evidence of my good fruits for world consumption in the name of Jesus (Luke 6: 43-44).

78. I will sing a joyful song unto the Lord because He has redeemed me and has glorified Himself in my life (Isaiah 44:23).

79. My heart rejoices in the Lord, because He has granted me my heart desires and made me smile at my enemies forever in Jesus name (1 Samuel 2:1).

80. I speak blessing onto my life to silence my enemies. They will find nothing to say about me, so shall it be in the mighty name of Jesus (Nehemiah 5:8).

81. My set time has come to be favored; therefore, I speak to every difficult problem in my life that has refused to leave me alone to leave NOW in Jesus name (Psalm 103:13).

82. In the name of Jesus Christ of Nazareth, I declare that every Jordan blocking my destiny, delaying my moving forward into prosperity in my life is cross over now. (Joshua 3:1).

83. I have been spread abroad like the four wind of heaven. God has sent me for glory to the nation which plunders me and anyone who touches me has touched the apple of God's eyes declares the Lord of host and I believe (Zechariah 2: 6-8).

84. No matter how negative and useless people perceive my progress, God has already taken control and it is well. I will excel in Jesus name. (Nehemiah 4: 3-7).

85. I prophesier to my life that, the spirit that wake Jesus Christ from the dead lives in me and has change every unquenchable situation pending in my life in the mighty name of Jesus (Romans 8:11).

86. And Jabez (his name mean pain) was honorable than all his brothers BUT his name disqualifies him. From today any BUT in my LIFE (name others if desired) is quenched by the power of the Holy Spirit to be dead NOW in Jesus precious name (1 Chronicles 4:9-10).

87. Until God opens your understanding you cannot comprehend consistencies. I declare my understanding in God's word be open NOW in the name of Jesus (Luke 24: 45).

88. By faith I speak healing into my life, any ancestral curses and infirmities are healed. Like the woman who by her faith touched the herm of Jesus garment and was healed (Luke 5:25- 29).

89. I will sing responsively, praising and giving God thanks because HE is super good and HIS mercies endures forever and ever toward me and my family (Ezra 3: 11).

90. I declare that, God has remembered me and showed me kindness as king David showed kindness to Mephibosheth (2 Samuel 9:1-10).

91. I believe in the name of Jesus, although life seems to be stagnant, I am coming out like David, who was nothing in his family but there was a turn-around in his life. (1 Samuel 17:17-18).

92. In the name of Jesus Christ of Nazareth, I am rising up to take over all my possessions today because; God has put fear unto my enemies who shall tremble in anguish because of me. (Deuteronomy 2: 24-25).

93. I will rejoice, praise and give God thanks always, in spite of all the situations I have been through God has delivered and blessed me. (1Thessalonians 5:16-18).

94. I am set free because of Christ and I cannot be entangled by any more yoke. I am liberated through the blood of Jesus. (Galatians 5:1).

95. I rejoice because my sorrows and burdens are taken away today. God is bringing me out of captivity to prosperity, praise and fame. (Zephaniah 3: 18-19).

96. In the name of Jesus, my children and I (mention names) are covered and the enemies cannot harm us. We will pass through their midst with great victory because of the blood of Jesus. (Luke 4:29-30).

97. I am a child of God who is not afraid because I have receive the spirit of adoption to overcome all thing especially FEAR. (Romans 8:14-15).

98. No enemy can trouble me because I bear in my body the mark of Christ Jesus. For this reason I walk in boldness and joy. (Galatians 6:17).

99. I declare in the name of Jesus that favor is mine because God has said it and it is established. My enemies will see me and favor me everywhere I go (Exodus 3:21).

100. In the name of Jesus, I am claiming my possession because I am a covenant daughter. (Exodus 6: 8).

101. I declare over me and my family's lives that from today we are free from all burden and stagnancy. The York is broken through the blood of Jesus HALLELUJA (Galatians 5:1).

102. I covered my tomorrow in the blood of Jesus, no evil shall be-fall any member in my household.(James 4:14).

103. I will surely cloth myself with the blessing of God as an ornament. It shall also be bind on me and my children and children's children because God does not lie and His promise shall come to pass in my life in the mighty name of Jesus. (Isaiah 49: 18).

104. The grace of God is working for me, I believe God is going to perform miracle in my life, which will shock many nations. Father let your will be done in my life, Amen. (Habakkuk 1:5).

105. My life is blessed because the word of God says so. It took the word to change my life for the better and nothing can change the blessings of God upon my life in Jesus name. (Genesis 1: 26-31 & Hebrew 11:3).

106. My destiny has change for the best because I diligently seek God in FAITH and I will not weary in faith till the end of my life. (Hebrews 11:6).

107. My tongue will bring me to my prosperity because I will not hesitate to declare blessing into your life. I will tame your tongue from destroying me and my love ones blessings in Jesus name (James 3:8).

108. I am the son of the living God; no devil can inflame my flesh. (Galatians 3:20)

109. God loves me and I will never lack. In Jesus name (John 17:20).

110. It took Nehemiah's obedience to build the walls which led to the move of God bringing the captives from Babylon to Jerusalem. Obedience is the key to prosperity. Holy Spirit, help me to be obedient, for God to honor His words in my life (Nehemiah 7:1-6).

111. In the name of Jesus, I declare, my hands will labor to gain multiple profits, it will not be idle. (Proverbs 14:23).

112. In the name of Jesus I declare, I am rich because God has given me the hidden

treasures of riches in secret places. None of my children will be poor and this shall be according to the word of God. (Isaiah 45: 3).

113. "If I can touch the herm of His garment I will be heal". Just like the woman with the issue of blood for twelve years. Speak prosperity into my life and be prosperous. I will release my faith to receive my healing in Jesus name. (Matthew 9:21).

114. Father I thank you for the great and effective opportunity doors that you have open for me and my family (mention names) (1 Corinthians 16: 9).

115. I am a special person, a blessed generation with royalty chosen by God. I have been brought to His marvelous light through Jesus Christ His son. (1 Peter 2:9).

116. I decree and declare that my faith in God will usher me new strength and boldness to get to my divine destiny as King David. (1 Samuel 17:50-51).

117. I am of good cheer because I am in Christ Jesus the only son of God; this has made me to overcome the world. (John 16: 33).

118. I believe God's word brings light to the lost and needy. So let God be true and all men be lie in my life. (Romans 3:4).

119. I declare that my children and I are of the seed of God, we have overcome the wicked plans of the enemies because greater is our Heavenly Father who has delivered us from them all. (1 John 4:4).

120. In the name of Jesus I confess that my FAITH in Christ Jesus has made me to overcome the world. I am VICTORIOUS! (1 John 5:4).

121. In the name of Jesus, today I have overcome fear because God gave me the power to love and to control myself from things that will make me loose focus on what God has for me. (2Timothy 1:7).

122. I decree and declare that my family is safe in the name of Jesus. I speak in faith because God has set the solidarity in my families, not only that, HE also brought us OUT of bondage. (Psalm 68:6).

123. My confidence and trust is in the Lord, so am not afraid of what the enemy might bring. In

the name of Jesus I will remain rooted and will always yield fruits and can NEVER be uprooted. (Jeremiah 17:7-8).

124. Father Lord, I ask for wisdom, knowledge and the ability to do your will to bring change to the needy in the name of Jesus. (2 Chronicles 1:10).

125. I decree and declare in Jesus name, God will stair up the hearts of my destiny helpers to release good proclamation to my life (mention the areas you want God to visit your needs) (Ezra1:1).

126. I put on my breastplate of righteousness, nothing can enslave me any more. Anything that entangled me is release in the blood of Jesus. (Ephesians 6:14).

127. I believe that the grace and favor of God has come upon me and my life is about to change in the mighty name of Jesus just like queen Esther. (Esther 2:17).

128. Lord, I thank you for the faith and boldness you have given me to triumph over my enemies to take what belong to me like Joshua and Caleb. (Numbers 14: 6-9).

129. In the name of Jesus I will peruse my destiny, I will NEVER be frustrated and discourage no matter the distractions I encounter.
(Ezra 4: 4-5).

130. Heavenly Father, I am thankful for the change of my name which is endorsed with blessings. I am fruitful and I will keep multiplying to the glory of God, nations and kings shall proceed for me in the mighty name of Jesus.
(Genesis 35:10-11).

131. Am grateful oh Lord; for the spirit of appreciation for all your goodness and not grumbling of the things am yet to receive. Thank you Jesus (Exodus 16:3-4).

132. I decree I am bless in the name of Jesus and I shall not look at the things or troubles I see, they are temporal but I will pursue in the things not seen for eternal (2 Corinthians 4:18).

133. I declare that I am blessed daily. I will press towards my blessings and nothing can stop me or make me go back like Ruth (Ruth 1:15-18).

134. Lord I thank you for honoring me and setting me above my peers and changing my destiny. It's a new day for me (Jeremiah 1:10).

135. The test of my faith has produced patience and by the grace of God I lack nothing. I am complete in Jesus name (James 3:4).

136. I will forever sing praises to you mighty God, because I have gained victory through your marvelous deeds and I am grateful. (Psalm 98:1).

137. I decree and declare that no man, woman or spirit that is not of God can stand against me in the name of Jesus because my God has put fear upon them (Deuteronomy 11:25).

138. Holy Spirit from today help me to be more obedient to the word of God. Obedience brings blessings and that is what I need in my life (Ruth 3: 3-7).

139. In the name of Jesus, I will lift my eyes up to the Lord and I know because of my FAITH my blessings will not pass me by. (Genesis 22:13).

140. Father, I thank you for making me become a partaker of your saved souls. I have laid away all filthiness and the wickedness in Jesus name (James 1:21).

141. My hope is rest fully in the grace of God this will bring me the revelations of Jesus Christ to walk as a matured and good Christian (1 Peter 1:13).

142. I will strike and focus on the word of God to attain blessings because all that is in the world is of the flesh which will lead me to destroying my soul (1 John 2:15).

143. God bestowed His love unto me and called me His own. I am a child of God and blessed daily I am going higher and higher in Jesus name Amen (1 John 3:1).

144. I will give GOD thanks because I was created to do so. Blessings, glory, wisdom and power belongs to God for He has dealt with me well to His glory (Revelation 7:12).

145. Lord, I thank you for your protection power, grace and favor that you have bestowed upon me to tear down the plans of the enemy in my life. I am a winner like Gideon through the blood of Jesus. (Judges 6-25-27).

146. I decree and declare, I will be carefully committed to the things of God and heed to instructions to be blessed (1 Chronicles 10-7).

147. I am blessed beyond curse, favored and graced beyond disgrace. This I know there is nothing anyone can do or change what God has done in Jesus name (Numbers 23:8).

148. For this I asked of the Lord and He has surely blessed me. Thank you Jesus for the manifestation of my prayers. I give you all the glory in Jesus name Amen (1 Samuel 1:27).

149. By faith I declare my God will bring me to my place of heritage and blessings because His word never fails. I believe I am a WINNER in the mighty name of Jesus (Exodus 6:8).

150. I decree and declare that God has brought me out of unpleasant situations that put my life in bondage, my life is turn around for good (Jeremiah 31:8).

151. I am blessed because my God has given me His word to comfort and to help me. He also strengthens me when am weary (Isaiah 50:4).

152. My God has remembered ME (put your name there), all my stagnancy, hindrance and disgrace are wiped away. I am free, I will rejoice. Thank you Jesus (Genesis 30:22).

153. I declare that because the sovereign God has blessed me, He will multiply me and make my generation blessed and mighty in Jesus name (Isaiah 51:2).

154. God you are my healer and the lifter of my head, you did not put me to shame, you make me to rejoice in Jesus name (Psalm 30:1).

155. I have no doubt that God will not help me. My enemies will be destroyed and they shall wear-out like an old cloth, which will be eaten by moths in Jesus name. (Isaiah 50:9).

156. God has shown me His mercy and favored me in the sight of my peers. Glory to your oh Lord (Genesis 39:21).

157. Father Lord, I thank you and give you all the praise for giving me help from all my troubles (Psalm 60:11).

158. Lord I will forever declare that, is by your grace that I am alive and you will continuously be with me in Jesus name. (Psalm 124:1).

159. Wonders are your works that is why I praise you in all that you have done. My soul will sing and rejoice in your Holy name (Psalm 139:14).

160. I have learnt to put my trust in the Lord and He will NEVER disappoint me. I declare by the power of God that me and my children (mention their names) shall not be put to shame in Jesus name (Judges 12:2).

161. My God will use the negative things in my life to confine to positive and also for wonders. I shall be a blessing which will be a talked about in all generations to come in Jesus name (Joshua 2:1-21).

162. Father, I thank you for making my feet like the deer and also my ways perfect. You oh Lord have given me exceeding strength and power to live and to do your work in Jesus name (2 Samuel 22:33-34).

163. God has blessed me with the things I did not ask for. May His glorious name be praise forever (1 Kings 3:13).

164. I decree and declare that my God is about to do wonders in my life today in Jesus name (1 Samuel 12:16).

165. In the name of Jesus I believe that my God has expelled and disgraced anyone who stood on my way to possess my blessings (Joshua 23:5).

166. I decree that God's word concerning my life is true and I will live prosperous in the name of Jesus (2 Samuel 7:28).

167. I thank God for giving me rest and a peace of mind. His promise is fulfilled and has not failed. My faith is working for me. I am blessed daily (1 Kings 8:56).

168. God will remember me today and make my life brand new in Jesus name (Psalm 105:42).

169. God has remembered me and has performed good things in my life. My peace is still because He paved the way for me. (Jeremiah 33:14).

170. I waited for the promise of God almighty and it has gladdened my heart. (acts 1:4).

171. I declare that I will not stagger at the promises in my life but I will always walk in faith to receive my portion (Romans 4:20).

172. I will not weaver at the promise to receive but with violent faith I will receive my heart desires and to enjoy the blessings of God (Hebrews 10:23).

173. God has given me rest, this I am confident. I am successful in all my ways (Joshua 23:1).

174. I will rejoice all the time because God's plan for my life is to prosper and give me good

health. Today I take my strength back fully in Jesus name (Jeremiah 29:11).

175. I thank God for the power He gives me when am weak. His name will forever be praise in Jesus name (Isaiah 40:29).

176. I know my God can do all things and all His purpose can never fail in my life (Job 42:2).

177. I waited upon the Lord and He renewed my strength and gave me wings like an eagle. Am grateful, I will never faint because He is with me (Isaiah 40:31).

178. I declare that all the impossible situations in my life are made possible now because I have God who takes care of my needs. (Luke 18:27).

179. I have trusted in God with all my heart because I am of flesh and blood and do not have understanding of the spirit but God does and He protects me (Proverbs 3:5-6).

180. I declare I am blessed because I have taken refuge in the Lord almighty (Psalm 34:8).

181. I decree and declare that everything is at ease for me because my God is in control and nothing is too difficult for Him. (Jeremiah 32:17).

182. In the name of Jesus all my heavy burdens are taken away because the word of God says so (Matthew 11:28).

183. I know I am a winner because God's ways are not man's way and His doings cannot be understood (Isaiah 55:8).

184. I declare I am free from anxieties because Jesus has taken it all (1 Peter 5:7).

185. Father, I thank you for the insight of great and mighty things you have for my life in Jesus name (Jeremiah 33:3).

186. I give God praise because He has supplied all my needs through His only son Jesus. I have abundance in everything. (Philippians 4:19).

187. I decree that as for me, I will always have hope in abundance through the spirit of God that strengthens me in Jesus name (Psalm 71:14).

188. Lord, I thank you for doing a new thing in my life (name others) and throughout my generation in Jesus name (Isaiah 43:19).

189. I believe my God is so faithful to fail me, my heart will rejoice because He has called me

to enjoy all the heavenly blessing on earth in Jesus name (1 Thessalonians 2:4).

190. I declare that I will never be shaken in spite of all the negativity around me because I have set my Lord continuously before me. He will fulfil His words to me. I shall not be put to shame (Psalm16:8).

191. I declare that God Himself has defended and strengthened me, He is my salvation and I will not be afraid (Isaiah 12:2).

192. Lord I thank you for being faithful in your promises in my life. Surely you are trustworthy God (Psalm 145:13-14).

193. My needs are met because my father has favored me. There's more to come in Jesus name (Matthew 6:7).

194. I am a child of God because of the blood of Jesus. Old sins and life style have passed away. Behold God is doing great things in my life all eyes will see (2 Corinthians 5:17).

195. In Jesus name I declare that everything I say would be of the things of God that will bring success and prosperity to beautify my life (Matthew 15:17).

196. I am highly blessed and favored because God has establish my plans as I am committed to Him (Proverbs 16:33).

197. My heart will rejoice because God has given me peace, He has kept and blessed me and made my face shine. I am grateful oh Lord (Numbers 6:24-26).

198. I declare I have stopped relying on myself and begin to rely on God who has made me live and did not die in spite of all the trails I faced (2 Corinthians 1:9).

199. I believe God is alive, everlasting savior who does Wonders in my life everyday. He has finish my case (Jeremiah 10:10).

200. The faithfulness of God has endured me through thick and thin. He always provides my needs, I am a believer and a child of God (1 Corinthians 10:13).

201. I declare that the peace of God dwells within me and my family (mention names) and friends (names) in Jesus name. (Psalm 122:7-8).

202. I will finish my race and live in success through Christ who strengthens me in Jesus name. (2 Timothy 4:7-8).

203. I declare joy and peace in all situations, I will give God thanks continuously no matter where I am (1 Thessalonians 5: 16-18).

204. Lord, you are my strength, my rock and my savior, I will trust in you forever, with you my life is secured (Psalm 18:1-2).

205. I declare that me and my family are blessed beyond measure in Jesus name (1 Chronicles 17:27).

206. Blessed be your name my Lord because you turn my mourning to laughter and my sorrows to gladness. I believe there is more to come in Jesus name (Esther 9:22).

207. I declare that I will not encounter any troubles as I step out because Jesus has overcome it all on the cross for me (John 16:33).

208. I receive my strength and protection from God because He is faithful to His promises (2 Thessalonians 3:3).

209. I declare that I am enriched with Abrahamic blessings which allows me to be a point of contact to others in Jesus name (2 Corinthians 9:11).

210. Lord Jesus, I thank you for making my life a success. You promised not to put me to shame, indeed you have kept your word. I give you praise for what you have done and what you are about to do in my life. (Isaiah 54:4).

Reader's Personal Notes

I AM BLESSED DAILY
2016 CALENDER

Year of favour

JANUARY

M	T	W	T	F	S	S
				1	2	3
4	5	6	7	8	9	10
11	12	13	14	15	16	17
18	19	20	21	22	23	24
25	26	27	28	29	30	31

FEBRUARY

M	T	W	T	F	S	S
1	2	3	4	5	6	7
8	9	10	11	12	13	14
15	16	17	18	19	20	21
22	23	24	25	26	27	28
29						

MARCH

M	T	W	T	F	S	S
	1	2	3	4	5	6
7	8	9	10	11	12	13
14	15	16	17	18	19	20
21	22	23	24	25	26	27
28	29	30	31			

APRIL

M	T	W	T	F	S	S
				1	2	3
4	5	6	7	8	9	10
11	12	13	14	15	16	17
18	19	20	21	22	23	24
25	26	27	28	29	30	

MAY

M	T	W	T	F	S	S
						1
2	3	4	5	6	7	8
9	10	11	12	13	14	15
16	17	18	19	20	21	22
23	24	25	26	27	28	29
30	31					

JUNE

M	T	W	T	F	S	S
		1	2	3	4	5
6	7	8	9	10	11	12
13	14	15	16	17	18	19
20	21	22	23	24	25	26
27	28	29	30			

JULY

M	T	W	T	F	S	S
				1	2	3
4	5	6	7	8	9	10
11	12	13	14	15	16	17
18	19	20	21	22	23	24
25	26	27	28	29	30	31

AUGUST

M	T	W	T	F	S	S
1	2	3	4	5	6	7
8	9	10	11	12	13	14
15	16	17	18	19	20	21
22	23	24	25	26	27	28
29	30	31				

SEPTEMBER

M	T	W	T	F	S	S
			1	2	3	4
5	6	7	8	9	10	11
12	13	14	15	16	17	18
19	20	21	22	23	24	25
26	27	28	29	30		

OCTOBER

M	T	W	T	F	S	S
					1	2
3	4	5	6	7	8	9
10	11	12	13	14	15	16
17	18	19	20	21	22	23
24	25	26	27	28	29	30
31						

NOVEMBER

M	T	W	T	F	S	S
	1	2	3	4	5	6
7	8	9	10	11	12	13
14	15	16	17	18	19	20
21	22	23	24	25	26	27
28	29	30				

DECEMBER

M	T	W	T	F	S	S
			1	2	3	4
5	6	7	8	9	10	11
12	13	14	15	16	17	18
19	20	21	22	23	24	25
26	27	28	29	30	31	

Author' note.

As a believer, you have the power to say and receive whatever you want when you have faith in Christ. You receive because there has been a positive proclamation backing your faith. You must also remember that, our tongue is a very powerful weapon, which brings us to our blessings. Christ has set us free from all bondage so we must live likewise.

This book was inspired by Holy Spirit on the 7th of May 2015, it will help you in your daily declaration to bring blessing into your life. It will also change your life and bring you to victorious breakthroughs. As you declare BELIEVE in FAITH that, it is yours because without faith God cannot help you. You are coming out of all situations as you decree & declare in Jesus name. Amen

About the Author

Selina was born in 1973 in Ghana. She has dedicated her life in the things of God for a long time at Kharis ministries. By the grace of God had achieved MSc in Investigative Forensic Psychology and aspiring to become an investigator. She joined the British Red Cross as a volunteer in 2005 as a first Aider.

She is a woman of faith, who through her strong faith, got completely healed from stroke when she was paralyzed on the 6th March 2014. She has repositioned herself to pursue into evangelism and winning souls for Christ.

www.ingramcontent.com/pod-product-compliance
Lightning Source LLC
Chambersburg PA
CBHW071039080526
44587CB00015B/2688